The All About Series

All About ... Canadian Sports

Skiing

Barb McDermott and Gail McKeown

Reidmore Books

Reidmore Books Inc.

For more information contact
Nelson Thomson Learning,
1120 Birchmount Road,
Scarborough, Ontario,
M1K 5G4.
Or you can visit our
internet site at
http://www.nelson.com

Printed and bound in Canada
2 3 4 5 03 02 01 00

We acknowledge the financial support of the
Government of Canada through the
Book Publishing Industry Development Program (BPIDP)
for our publishing activities.

Canada

Canadian Cataloguing in Publication Data
McDermott, Barb.
All about Canadian sports : skiing

(All about series)
Includes index.
ISBN 1-896132-47-2

1. Downhill skiing–Canada–Juvenile literature. 2. Cross-country skiing–Canada–Juvenile literature. I. McKeown, Gail. II. Title. III. Series: McDermott, Barb. All about series.
GV854.8.C3M32 1999 j796.93′5′0971 C99-910771-2

About the Authors

Barb McDermott and Gail McKeown are highly experienced kindergarten teachers living in Ontario. Both hold Bachelor of Arts and Bachelor of Education degrees, Early Childhood diplomas, specialist certificates in Primary Education, and have completed qualification courses in Special Education. As well, Gail has a specialist certificate in Reading and Visual Arts, and Barb has one in Guidance.

Content Reviewer

James Lloyd Mandigo, Faculty of Physical Education and Recreation, University of Alberta

Sports Historian

Dr. PearlAnn Reichwein, Assistant Professor, Faculty of Physical Education and Recreation, University of Alberta

Credits

Editorial: Leah-Ann Lymer, Scott Woodley, David Strand
Illustration, design and layout: Bruno Enderlin, Leslieanna Blackner Au

Photo Credits

Cover photo: Paul Morrison/ Viewpoints West
Stamp photo: Kaj Svensson/ Viewpoints West

Page

1 Randy Lincks/Image Network Inc.
3 Kaj Svensson/Viewpoints West
5 Jan Greve/Scanfoto-Royal Norwegian Embassy
7 Edmonton Ski Club
9 Snow Valley
11 Paul Morrison/Viewpoints West
13 Brian Sprout/Image Network Inc.
15 Randy Lincks/Image Network Inc.
17 Mike Desjardins/Viewpoints West
19 Paul Morrison/Viewpoints West
21 Canadian Ski Marathon
23 Frank Gasparik
25 Snow Valley
27 Paul Morrison/Viewpoints West

We have made every effort to identify and credit the sources of all photographs, illustrations, and information used in this textbook. Reidmore Books appreciates any further information or corrections; acknowledgment will be given in subsequent editions.

Table of Contents

(All about what's in the book)

Introduction

(All about the beginning)

Sports are games that people play to have fun.

Sports help people to stay healthy.

Sports can teach people how to work together.

Sports are fun to watch.

Skiing is 1 of the sports that Canadians do.

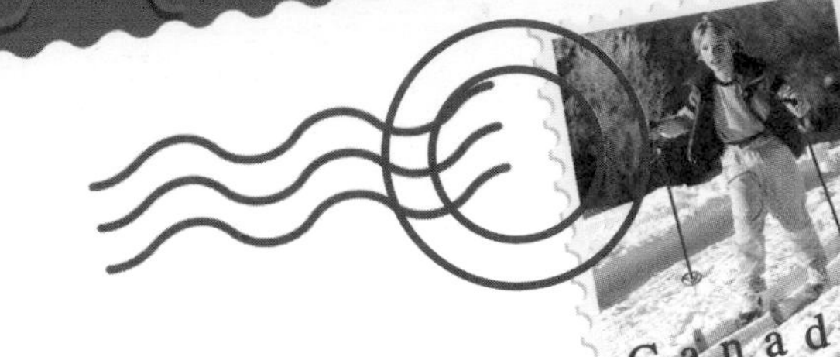

Downhill Skiing Is a Fun Sport

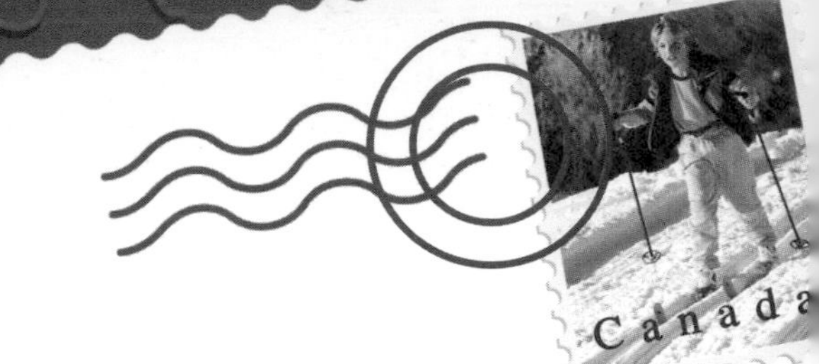

Introduction

(All about skiing)

Skiing is a winter sport.

Two popular types of skiing are downhill skiing and cross-country skiing.

Downhill skiing is done outside on a hill or mountain.

Cross-country skiing can be done on special trails, or wherever there is space outside.

Skiers use special skis and poles to move across the snow.

Cross-Country Skiing on Special Trails

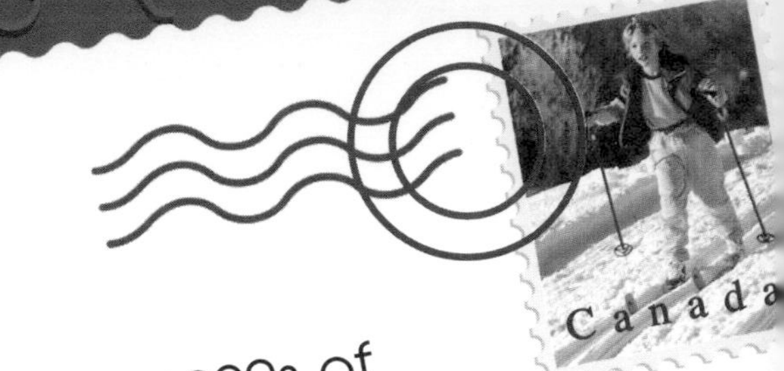

History

(All about how skiing began)

Skiing began in **northern Europe** and in **Asia** 1000s of years ago.

Skis that are 1000s of years old have been found in **bogs** in Norway and Sweden.

Very old pictures and rock **carvings** of skiing have been found in Russia and Norway.

Very old Chinese writings talk about skiing.

The 1st skis may have been made from animal bones.

A 4000-Year-Old Rock Carving of a Skier in Norway

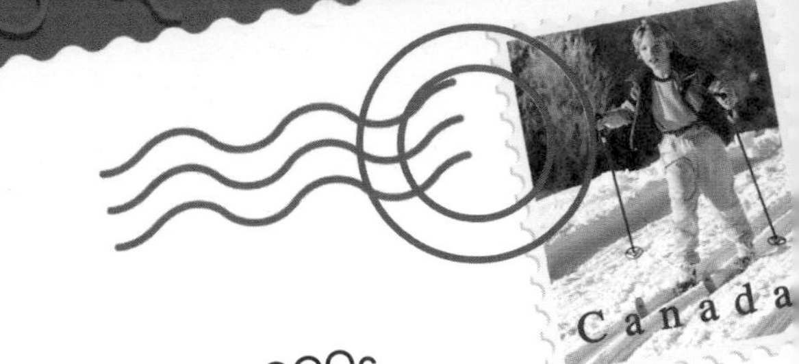

History

(All about how skiing began)

The **Vikings** who came to Newfoundland in the 900s may have been the 1st skiers in Canada.

People from Sweden, Norway, and Finland brought skiing to Canada in the 1800s.

Ski **clubs** formed 1st in Revelstoke, British Columbia in 1891 and Montreal, Quebec in 1904.

The 1st ski **competition** in Canada was in Rossland, British Columbia in 1898.

Ready for a Ski Race in Banff

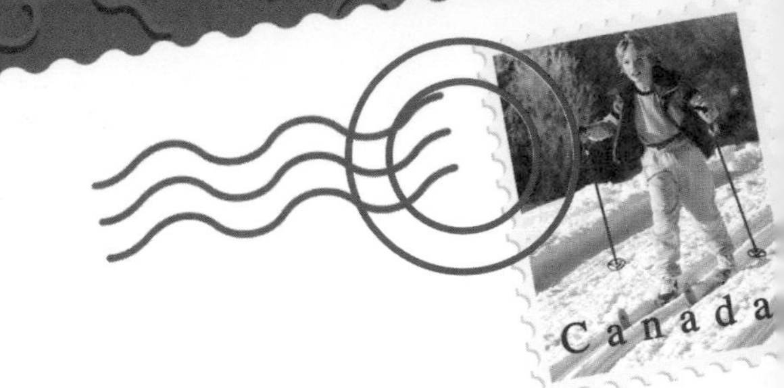

Uniform
(All about what skiers wear)

Skiers wear a ski suit to stay warm.

Skiers wear warm clothing under the ski suit.

Skiers wear thick, warm gloves and socks.

Skiers wear toques and sometimes short scarves.

Some skiers wear goggles or sunglasses and sunscreen to **protect** themselves from the sun.

Skiers Dress to Stay Warm

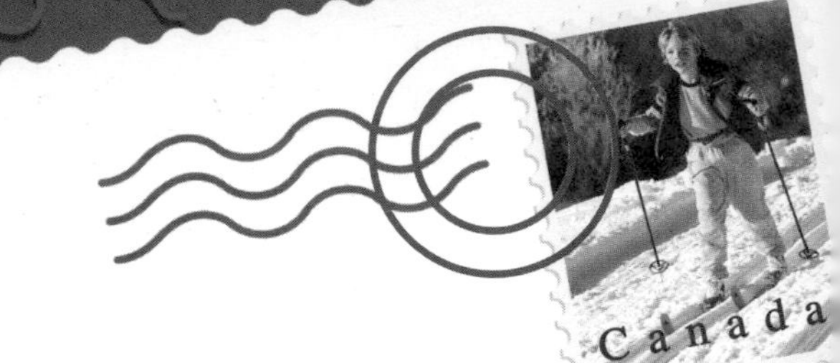

Equipment
(All about what is used to ski)

Skiers wear special ski boots.

Ski boots are flat on the bottom.

Ski boots have padded ankles inside.

Ski boots are heavy and are made of thick, hard plastic.

Skiers must wear ski boots that fit properly, or they will hurt themselves.

Ski Boots Must Fit Properly

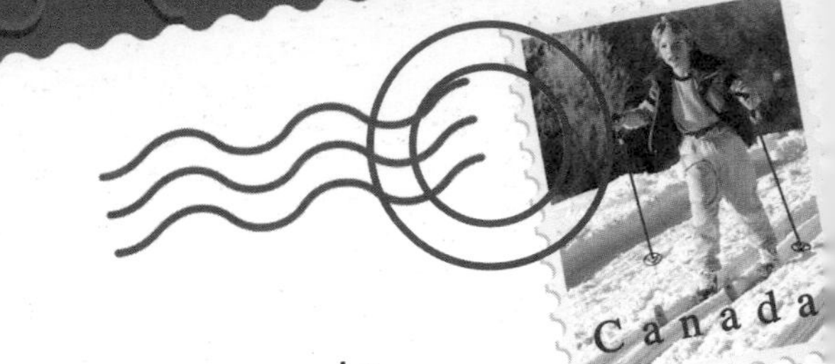

Equipment

(All about what is used to ski)

Skiers attach wooden or plastic skis to their ski boots.

Bindings keep the ski boots on the skis.

Skiers use 2 ski poles.

Ski poles have hand grips, straps, and a small **disk** at the bottom to keep the pole from sinking too far into the snow.

Skis and ski poles come in different lengths because skiers must choose the best length for their own height.

Skiers Use Poles

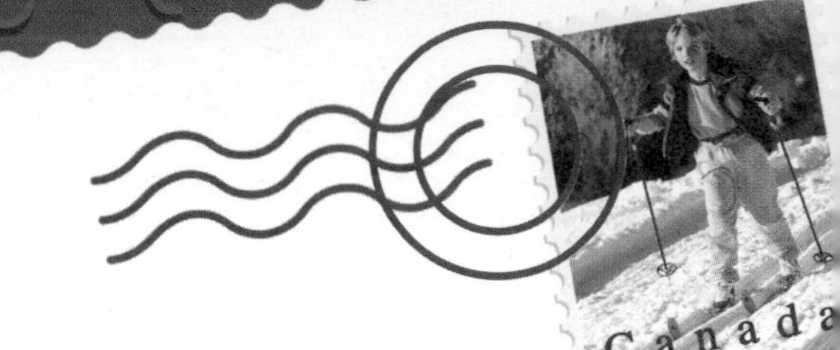

Facility

(All about where to ski)

Downhill skiing is enjoyed in ski **resorts** across Canada.

Ski resorts have **ski lifts** to carry downhill skiers up hills and mountains.

Ski resorts have ski teachers.

Many ski resorts and parks make special trails for cross-country skiers.

Cross-country skiers can also make their own trails if they know the area is safe.

A Ski Lift

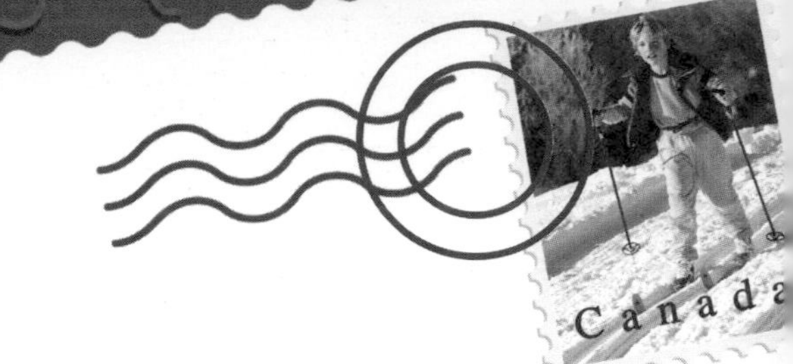

Downhill Races
(All about downhill races)

Some people like to **compete** in ski races.

In a downhill ski race, 1 skier at a time must pass through every gate on the **course.**

A gate is made of poles with flags.

Skiers are allowed to knock down poles as they pass through the gates.

The winner is the skier who passes through every gate and finishes the course the fastest.

Some Skiers Like to Race

Slalom Races

(All about slalom races)

In a slalom race, 1 skier at a time skis down a hill in a zig-zag pattern.

Each skier must pass through 45 to 75 gates.

Each skier must do a lot of twisting and turning as they ski the course.

Each skier must ski 2 different courses in a slalom race.

The winner is the skier with the fastest **combined** time on the 2 courses.

Skiing in a Zig-Zag Pattern

Canadian Ski Marathon

(All about a cross-country skiing race)

The Canadian Ski Marathon has a 170 km cross-country ski course in Quebec.

The course is divided into 10 sections, and the skiers win medals depending on how many sections they have finished.

Bronze medals go to skiers who finish the 170 km course.

Silver medals go to skiers who finish the 170 km course while carrying a 5 kg pack on their back.

Gold medals go to skiers who finish the 170 km course while carrying a heavy pack and camping out overnight.

Canada

Canadian Ski Marathon

Canadian Birkebeiner Ski Festival

(All about a cross-country skiing festival)

Over 2000 cross-country skiers come to the Canadian Birkebeiner Ski Festival in Edmonton, Alberta each year.

The Canadian Birkebeiner Ski Festival has many activities for cross-country skiers of all ages and abilities.

The main event at this festival is the Torskeklubben Birkebeiner.

The Torskeklubben Birkebeiner is a race in which each skier tries to ski 55 km with a $5\frac{1}{2}$ kg pack on his or her back.

The fastest skier to finish the 55 km course wins.

Canadian Birkebeiner Ski Festival

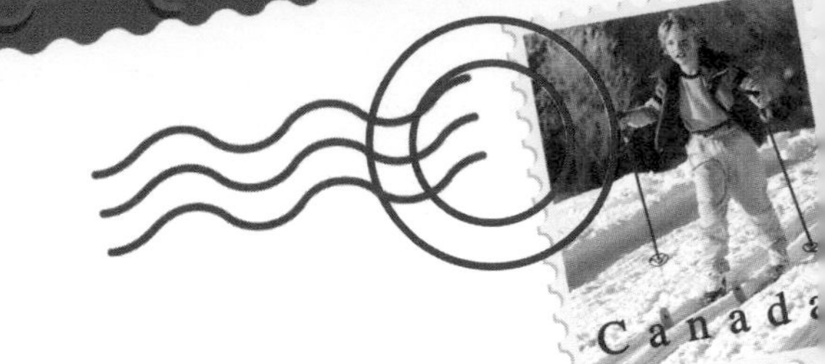

Skills

(All about what skiing teaches)

Skiers learn how to move their arms and legs together.

Skiers learn how to look for danger and keep away from it.

Skiers learn to control how quickly they go down a hill or mountain.

Skiers learn how to ski long distances without getting tired.

Learning How to Ski

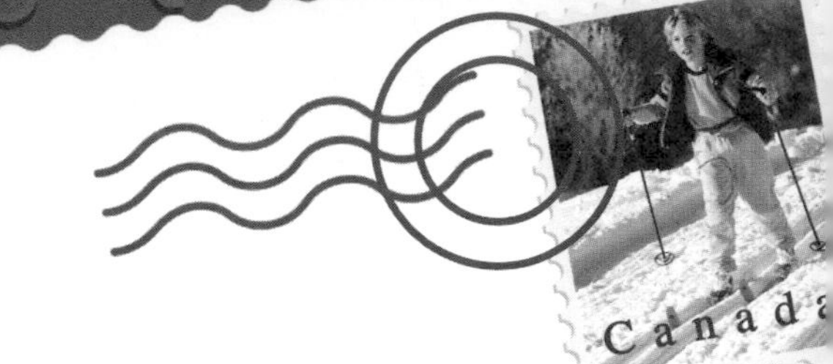

Summary
(All about the ending)

Canadians ski to have fun and stay healthy.

Skiing came from northern Europe and Asia 1000s of years ago.

Skiers use skis and ski poles to move across snow.

Skiing is an amazing sport ... enjoyed by Canadians!

Canadians Enjoy Skiing

Glossary
(All about what the words mean)

Asia (page 4)
Asia is an area that includes the countries of China, Japan, and Russia.

bogs (page 4)
Bogs are areas of soft, wet land.

carvings (page 4)
A carving is something that has pictures or letters cut into it.

combined (page 18)
In a slalom race, skiers add their time from the 1st course to their time from the 2nd course to decide whether they have won the race. In other words, they win depending on how fast their combined time was.

compete (page 16)
To compete is to work hard to win something that other people also want.

competition (page 6)
A competition is a contest where people try to win something.

course (page 16)
A course is a path created for a certain purpose.

disk (page 12)
A disk is a thin, round, flat object.

northern Europe (page 4)
Northern Europe is an area that includes the countries of Denmark, Norway, Sweden, Finland, and Iceland.

protect (page 8)
To protect something is to defend it from harm.

resorts (page 14)
A resort is a place where people go to relax and have fun.

ski lifts (page 14)
A ski lift is a set of chairs hanging from a cable. The cable pulls the chairs to the top of the ski hill or mountain.

Vikings (page 6)
Vikings were people from northern Europe (such as Norway and Iceland) who explored in ships along the eastern coast of Canada around 1000 AD. Vikings had to travel about 3000 km by ocean to reach Canada.